TENNIS

D1404110

PLAY THE GAME

TENNIS

SIMON LEE

BLANDFORD

First published in Great Britain in 1988
by Ward Lock; revised 1993 by Blandford,
Villiers House, 41-47 Strand, London, WC2N 5JE

Reprinted 1993. A Cassell Imprint.

Designed by Anita Ruddell
Figure drawings by Jerry Malone
Other illustrations by Peter Bull Art

Text set in Helvetica
by Hourds Typographica, Stafford, England
Printed and bound in Great Britain by
The Bath Press, Avon

British Library Cataloguing in Publication Data
Lee, Simon
    Play the game
    1. Lawn Tennis
    I. Title
    796.342

ISBN 0 7137 2413 7

Acknowledgments

The author and publishers would like to
thank Colorsport for supplying the
photographs reproduced in this book.

**Frontispiece: The great Martina
Navratilova, serving her way to yet another
victory at Wimbledon.**

CONTENTS

Foreword   6

History & development of tennis   8
Equipment & terminology   14
The game – a guide   30
Rules clinic   39
Technique   46

Useful addresses   77

Rules clinic index   79

General index   80

FOREWORD

Lawn tennis in Britain is going through one of its healthiest periods. Thanks to world superstars like Boris Becker, Ivan Lendl, Hana Mandlikova and Gabriela Sabatini, British youngsters are taking up the sport in large numbers, in the hope of emulating their idols. At grass roots level, these newcomers are being encouraged away from the friendly game in the local park and into the world of competitive tennis.

For so long we have lacked that essential competitive edge amongst our top players; of course we have had exceptions like Virginia Wade, Mark Cox and Buster Mottram, but in all honesty we have not been a match for the top Australians, Americans, and, in recent years, Europeans. Hopefully that will change in the years to come as the new breed of young British tennis player makes the breakthrough into the top flight.

For those youngsters starting to develop their game there can be no finer starting place than this book in the Ward Lock *Play the Game* series. The book is comprehensive yet, at the same time, easy to read without getting too technical.

The history of the game is chronicled from the day Major Clopton Wingfield developed his variation of tennis, which went under the rather weird and wonderful name of 'sphairistiké'. The game has come a long way since then and is now one of the world's leading sports. In terms of its commercial value, there are few to rival it.

If you have dreams of winning Wimbledon, or representing your country in the Davis Cup or Wightman Cup, then you have to start somewhere, and *Play the Game: Tennis* is a sound starting point.

FOREWORD

After offering a fascinating history of the game, the book introduces you to the equipment needed to play the game, and its guide to tennis terminology is particularly useful. The rules of the game are detailed in a simple, but comprehensive way, and for those rules that need that extra bit of clarification, the author has cleverly catered for them in a question and answer section called the 'Rules Clinic'.

The final section shows you how to play the game of lawn tennis. Any youngster taking up the game for the first time will undoubtedly have his or her own hero and will try to mould their game on that particular player. But, before you can do that, you must master the basic arts of service, ground strokes and volleys. *Play the Game: Tennis* shows you how to play all these shots, and in a simple way. It gets you started with the basics: thereafter it is up to you. The more you play the better you will become, and the better you get, the more you will start developing some of your own techniques and points of style.

No book can turn you into the world's number one player – that is up to you. *Play the Game: Tennis* can, however, start you on that road to the top, and it will certainly lead you to more success and enjoyment in a wonderful game.

David Lloyd

HISTORY &
DEVELOPMENT OF
TENNIS

Tennis in its indoor form dates from the eleventh century, when a game called *jeu de paume* was played in French monasteries. That original game forms the basis of 'real' or 'royal' tennis, as played today. The first strung racket is believed to have been introduced in the fifteenth century by an Italian priest, Antonio da Scalo, who also wrote a general treatise about all ball games, including tennis.

As an outdoor game, field tennis was mentioned in the English journal, *Sporting Magazine*, in 1793, when it was referred to as field tennis. This could well have been the same game as long tennis, which was mentioned in a *Book of Games and Sports* eighty years later.

Real, or royal tennis, was a game for the aristocracy, but lawn tennis, which became popular during Queen Victoria's reign, was a game for the middle class, who adapted real tennis into an outdoor game.

It is known that a Spaniard, J.B. Perera, and Major Harry Gem, clerk to the Birmingham Magistrates, played an outdoor version of tennis on the lawn of Perera's house in Ampton Road, Edgbaston, Birmingham, in 1859. They later played on a lawn adjacent to the Manor House Hotel, Leamington Spa, where, in 1872, along with Dr Frederick Haynes and Dr Arthur Tomkins, they formed the first known lawn tennis club, the Leamington Club. However, the sport was not called lawn tennis at the time but was referred to as either pelota or lawn rackets.

In 1874 Major Walter Clopton Wingfield attempted to commercialize the game, which he had now re-christened 'sphairistiké', by publishing a book of rules under the title *New and Improved Court for Playing the Ancient Game of Tennis*. Imagine Desmond Lynam on a Saturday afternoon saying: 'And now it's over to Wimbledon for a bit of sphairistiké!' Fortunately for Des, and the sporting world in general, it was soon re-named lawn tennis.

Wingfield had introduced his new game during a Christmas party at a country house in Nantclwyd, Wales, the previous year. Unlike the rectangular court at Leamington, Wingfield's court was shaped like an hour-glass, tapering at the net! A bust of Major Wingfield, bearing the inscription 'The Founder of Lawn Tennis' can be found in the offices of the Lawn Tennis Association.

Wingfield was, interestingly, a direct relation of John Wingfield, the English gaoler for Charles d'Orléans, a grandson of Charles VI of France, himself an enthusiastic tennis player.

Lawn tennis was seen as a game that could be played by both men and women, hence its rapid increase in popularity. But Wingfield's court and basic rules left a lot to be desired.

Later in 1874, the first game of lawn tennis ever to take place in the United States was played by Dr James Dwight and F.R. Sears.

The All-England Croquet Club had been founded in 1868, and two years later opened at its headquarters in Worple Road, Wimbledon. In 1875 the club agreed to set aside part of the ground for the playing of lawn tennis and badminton. Within a few months the first standardized set of lawn tennis rules had been drawn up, and by the end of that year the first American club was opened at Staten Island.

Over a short period, lawn tennis had rapidly grown in popularity as a leisure pursuit.

The All-England Croquet Club changed its name in 1877 to incorporate the words 'lawn tennis', and in 1882 the word croquet was dropped. It was reinstated in 1899 when the club assumed its present name, the All-England Lawn Tennis and Croquet Club.

In June 1877 the committee agreed to organize a championship to be called the Championships in Lawn Tennis, which was to herald the start of the most famous tennis event in the world – the Wimbledon Championships.

Between 9 and 19 July 1877 twenty-one players fought out the championship, and the first winner was Spencer William Gore who beat William Marshall 6-1 6-2 6-4 in front of just 200 spectators. A far cry from the 15,000 that fill the Centre Court today!

The United States Lawn Tennis Association was founded in 1881 and later that year they organized their first championships at Newport, Rhode Island.

Men's singles and doubles were held.

The first women's singles at Wimbledon took place in 1884, while it was 1887 before they were introduced into the US Championships. Men's doubles also officially made its debut at Wimbledon in 1884, while the first official women's and mixed doubles were not held until 1913. The first French Championships were held in 1891 but were open only to members of French clubs and did not become an international event until 1925. The fourth leg of the Grand Slam, the Australian Championships, were inaugurated in 1905.

Lawn tennis is currently making a comeback as an Olympic sport but it was included in the first modern Games at Athens in 1896 and at every celebration up until 1924.

Tennis had certainly spread internationally in its early years, and in 1883 the first match between the British Isles and United States took place at Wimbledon. The following year three Americans became the first of many to make an assault on the

TENNIS

Wimbledon championships. This international appeal led to the founding of the Davis Cup, the game's most important international team event. The United States easily beat the British Isles at Boston, Massachusetts in 1900 to win the first trophy. The winning captain was Dwight F. Davis, the man who presented the trophy.

To confirm the sport's appeal all over the world the International Lawn Tennis Federation was formed in March 1913. The majority of the twelve founder members were European, including Russia, but other founders included South Africa and Australasia.

A significant year in tennis history was 1922. In that year seeding was first introduced into the US Championships. (Two years later it was first used at Wimbledon). But 1922 was also a special year in the All-England Club's history. Firstly, the club moved from Worple Road to its present home at Church Road. Secondly, the 1922 championships were the first to be conducted on a knockout basis.

From the time of the inauguration of the championships in 1877, they had been conducted on a challenge basis. In other words, the defending champion(s) had only to play one match to retain his or her title. The challenger was, however, found as the result of a knockout tournament. Consequently it meant that such men as William Renshaw, Reggie and Laurie Doherty and Tony Wilding were installed as champion and were difficult to remove. Renshaw held the title for six consecutive years.

The abolition of the challenge system heralded a succession of new names in the tennis world. Four Frenchmen dominated the game in both their own country and at Wimbledon in those early years – Jean Borotra, Henri Cochet, Rene Lacoste and Jacques Brugnon. Collectively they became known as 'The Four Musketeers'. Between them they won the men's singles at Wimbledon six times in the first eight years

after the abolition of the challenge system. Their domination was broken in the late 1930s when Britain produced its own hero – Fred Perry, the last British men's singles champion at Wimbledon.

In 1938 the American Donald Budge became the first man to achieve the Grand Slam, the winning of the four major tournaments in one year – Wimbledon, the United States, France and Australia. Since then only one other man has performed the feat; Australia's Rod Laver, who won all four titles in both 1962 and 1969.

Women have also had their heroines over the years; Lottie Dod, the youngest ever Wimbledon champion at the age of fifteen, dominated the women's game in the early years. She was later to become an outstanding champion at golf as well. Suzanne Lenglen of France flew the flag for the fair sex while the Four Musketeers were dominating the men's game, but the inter-war years of women's tennis were dominated by Helen Wills-Moody of the United States, who won the women's title at Wimbledon a record eight times.

After the war, Maureen Connolly, affectionately known as 'Little Mo', became the first woman to perform the Grand Slam, in 1953. Margaret Court is the only other women to have won all four titles in the same season, although Martina Navratilova has held all four major titles simultaneously, though without winning all four in the same year. Surprisingly Billie Jean King, winner of a record twenty Wimbledon titles, never performed the Grand Slam.

The big four championships were strictly amateur events. Many top players, however, particularly in the 1950s and 1960s, left the amateur game to join the increasing number of professional tours that were being established. Professional tennis has been in when Rothmans sponsored a tournament at

Jim Courier in action at Wimbledon 1992.

introduced to the Wimbledon championships the following year. Never again will Wimbledon see a scoreline like: 22-24, 1-6, 16-14, 6-3, 11-9. That was the score in the men's singles when Pancho Gonzales beat Charlie Pasarell in 1969.

For a long time American and Australian players dominated both men's and women's tennis, but in the 1970s that began to change as the Europeans came to the fore.

The Davis Cup, which had, like the other big tournaments, been run on a challenge basis since its inception, became a knockout event in 1973. New nations such as Romania, Czechoslovakia and Sweden emerged and became a threat to the 'big two'. Stars like Ilie Nastase, Bjorn Borg, Ivan Lendl and, more recently, West Germany's Boris Becker emerged to rival Jimmy Connors and John McEnroe of the United States.

Bjorn Borg's post-war record of winning the men's singles at Wimbledon five years in succession is unlikely to be beaten in the foreseeable future. But in Martina Navratilova, women's tennis has Borg's equal. In fact she can go one better: she has won the ladies' title six years in succession and eight times altogether.

At one time lawn tennis, by definition, was only played on grass. Today, while still retaining its name, it is played on a variety of surfaces. There is the artificial surface, turf, the hard court (concrete or shale) and, of course, tennis is played indoors on wood or concrete covered by an artificial mat which resembles grass.

Beckenham, Kent. It did not take long for the sport to develop into the big money-spinner it is today.

The sport went 'open' in 1968, when the British Hard Court Championships at Bournemouth staged tennis's first Open event. Later that year Rod Laver returned to Wimbledon as a professional and won his fourth title.

The tie-break, which eliminates lengthy sets, was first used in 1970 and was existence since 1926 when, amongst others, Suzanne Lenglen turned professional. But in 1963 the first signs of commercialism and sponsorship of today's game were seen

Some players are specialists on one type of surface. For example, Ivan Lendl is probably the best male player in the world at the moment, but he seems to have a 'mental block' when it comes to playing on grass. His record at Wimbledon does not do justice to his talent.

For nearly 100 years there has been little change in the size of the tennis court, height of net and size of ball. The current dimensions of the court (23.77m [78ft] ×

10.97m [36ft]) were adopted in 1880, and two years later the net was standardized at a height of 0.91m (3ft) at the centre and 1.07m (3ft 6in) at the posts. The first court at the Leamington Club was 27.43m (90ft) × 10.97m × (36ft) with a net 1.22m (4ft) high.

It was more than 100 years before any legislation was made about the racket, in terms of either its size or construction. In 1977, however, double stringing became popular, and the International Tennis Federation finally made a specific recommendation by immediately outlawing this innovation.

Tennis is an inexpensive sport to take up. You can buy a racket fairly cheaply (there again, you can also pay a small fortune for one!), and the cost of hiring a court at your local park is nominal, particularly if there are four of you playing. Most municipal parks have concrete courts, thus keeping down the cost of maintaining grass courts.

Tennis is taught in most schools, and these days the game can be played all the year round because many leisure centres have indoor courts. Tennis coaches are based throughout Britain, and if you contact the Lawn Tennis Association they will put you in touch with one in your area. Once you feel ready to go on and play a better standard of tennis than against your pals in the local park, then you can join a local tennis club. Most clubs accept members at early ages, and for the betterment of the game players are encouraged to join a club as young as possible.

EQUIPMENT & TERMINOLOGY

Before we set about explaining the rules and telling you how to play tennis, you ought to familiarize yourself with the essential tennis equipment and get to know the court.

The court

As we said in the opening chapter, tennis is played on a variety of surfaces these days, not just grass. Climates often dictate the use of certain surfaces, and worldwide a selection of courts constructed of grass, sand, clay, asphalt, cement and shale can be found. In addition, indoor courts can be made of wood, nylon and rubber. However, the majority of courts you will find yourself playing on will be hard courts, generally constructed of concrete, and either painted (normally green) or covered in a fine shale. If the latter, do take care because a fall on a shale surface can cause a nasty grazing.

The court is rectangular and measures 23.77m (78ft) in length by 10.97m (36ft) wide. Within that area are two strips, one down each of the long sides of the court. These are 1.37m (4ft 6in) wide and known as the tramlines. They are only used in doubles play. In singles they have no use and any ball landing in the tramlines is out.

The court is divided into two halves by a net stretched across the width at the middle.

The net is 1.07m (3ft 6in) high at the supporting posts and 0.91m (3ft) at the centre.

The lines determining the outer sides of the court are called sidelines and those which determine the outer ends of the court are known as baselines. In addition to these lines there are three other markings in each *half* of the court.

A service line is marked parallel to the net and at a point 6.4m (21ft) from the net. The service line does not extend into the tramlines. Another line is then drawn from the centre of the net to the centre of the service line. This is called the centre service line. Two boxes have now been created and when serving, the ball must land in either of these boxes, depending on which side the service is made from.

The final court marking is at the middle of the baseline. It is a small mark indicating the middle of the baseline. Hardly surprising this mark is called the centre mark.

All court markings should be the same colour but they can vary in size. The centre service line must be 5cm (2in) wide, as must the centre mark (which is, in effect, an

The brilliant Andre Agassi demonstrating first class backhand technique.

Court dimensions

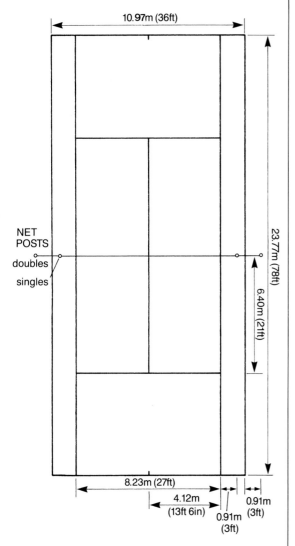

10.97m (36ft)

23.77m (78ft)

6.40m (21ft)

NET
POSTS

doubles

singles

8.23m (27ft)

4.12m
(13ft 6in)

0.91m
(3ft)

0.91m
(3ft)

extension of the centre service line). All other markings must be between 2.5–5cm (1–2in) except the baseline which can be up to 10cm (4in) wide.

Right, that's the court dealt with. But before we move on to the next section I think we ought to have a closer look at the net.

The two posts which support the net must be positioned 0.91m (3ft) outside the playing area. As there are two playing areas, one for singles and one for doubles, the supporting posts have therefore got a different position for each game. But both must be 0.91m (3ft) outside the court. Most major venues will have two different nets, one for singles play and one for doubles play. However, if only one net is used for both games then 'singles sticks' have to be used for the singles game. These are inserted in the ground 0.91m (3ft) from the sideline, and support the net at a height of 1.07m (3ft 6in).
    The net is supported by a cord or metal cable and covered by white tape. The net is adjustable and a handle at one of the posts is provided for this purpose. You will quite often see players testing the height of the net at the centre by standing one racket on end

The net

If the same net is used for doubles and singles play, 'singles sticks' should be put in place when the singles game is played. These are 1.07m (3ft 6in) high and are positioned 0.91m (3ft) outside the singles sidelines. The doubles posts are positioned 0.91m (3ft) outside the doubles sidelines.

singles
stick

post

height at centre
0.91m (3ft)

singles
stick

post

1.07m (3ft 6in)

Rackets

The traditional wooden racket.

The more modern composite metal racket.

and putting the head of another on top of it at right-angles. This is by no means accurate but, in the absence of any other means of checking the height, is a useful substitute.

You have now learned what we are going to play the game on, but what are we going to play it with?

The racket

As we said earlier, for more than 100 years there was no legislation governing the tennis racket – either its size or what it was made of. But now, there are certain limitations. The overall length of the frame, including the handle, must not exceed 81.28cm (32in) and the overall width should be no more than 31.75cm ($12\frac{1}{2}$in).

The head of the racket is strung with natural gut or an artificial material like nylon. The rules say that the hitting area must be flat and consist of a pattern of crossed strings connected to the frame. The stringing must be as uniform as possible and have the same density all over. The strung surface shall not exceed 39.3cm ($15\frac{1}{2}$in) in overall length or be greater than 29.21cm ($11\frac{1}{2}$in) wide.

Racket frames were traditionally made of wood and a great percentage of rackets are still wooden, particularly the very top quality type. However, in recent years aluminium – and graphite – framed rackets have become very popular. Rackets vary in weight according to personal preference, but the average is 368.55–396.90g (12–14oz).

The ball

The tennis ball is made of rubber and covered with wool or any acceptable man-made substitute, but it must not have stitched seams. When made, each ball should be pressurized so that when dropped on to a concrete surface from a height of 2.54m (100in) it will bounce to between 1.35–1.47m (53–58in). The diameter of the ball is between 6.35–6.67cm ($2\frac{1}{2}$–$2\frac{5}{8}$in) and

The ball

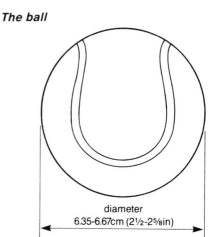

diameter
6.35-6.67cm (2½-2⅝in)

weight between 56.70–58.50g (2–2$\frac{1}{16}$oz). White balls are now uncommon as yellow has become the popular and accepted colour.

In major tournament play balls are kept refrigerated. Normally six balls are in play at any one time, and because they change pressure and shape through being constantly hit, the balls are changed at the end of the first seven games, and every nine thereafter.

Tennis shoes

It is important that your shoes should be (a) comfortable (b) lightweight and (c) ventilated.

Finally, clothing. As in all sports it is important to feel comfortable when playing tennis. Your feet need particular attention because they take some hammering during a game which, if it goes to five sets, can take a good three or four hours to complete.

Tennis shoes

A wide selection of tennis shoes (affectionately called 'trainers') are available in most shoe shops and sports goods shops. The prices vary from £15 to well over £50. Naturally, the funds available help you in making such a choice, but often shoes in the £20-30 range are as acceptable as those at the top end of the market.

These days they are made from very lightweight materials which put less strain on the feet. Believe me, at the end of three or four hours of tennis the feet and legs wish they were soaking in a nice warm bath rather than running round after a little yellow ball on a tennis court! Make sure any shoes you buy are ventilated.

Clothing

Again, tennis clothing comes in a wide range of prices. The important thing about clothing is to feel comfortable and have the freedom to move easily.

White was the traditional colour of tennis players' clothing for over 100 years, but the

Clothing

This is how you should dress for a game of tennis.

trend is to wear pastel-coloured clothing covered in patterns and motifs. Although Wimbledon still insists on a white base for shirts and shorts (or skirts).

Men wear shorts with pockets in which to put a spare ball when not in use, while women wear skirts, although some wear shorts. Skirts can also come with an internal pocket in which to house a ball.

The right choice of socks is important. You would be silly to wear a nylon pair to play tennis in. White towelling ones are far more practical.

If you perspire a lot, sweat bands, both for the wrist and head, are worth investing in. There is nothing worse than having a stream of sweat constantly rolling down your forehead and into your eyes.

You are well advised to take a towel on to court with you. A bottle of something cool to drink (but not fizzy) is also a good idea, and some talcum powder for those 'sweaty' hands will come in useful.

That's it. You now know what you are going to play on, you know what you are going to play with, and you know how to dress properly and sensibly. It's nearly time to learn how to play the game! But first of all, let's look at some tennis terms you will come across during the rest of the book and when you are playing and watching the game. Understanding the terms is just as important as understanding the rules.

The backhand shot

Goran Ivanisevic playing a backhand.

TERMINOLOGY

Ace   A serve which the receiver cannot get to and return is an ace. If he or she gets their racket to the ball but fails to return it, then it is NOT an ace, but just a good winning serve.

Advantage   If the score goes to deuce (see scoring on page 34) the next point won is known as advantage, and to the person who won the point.

Approach shot   A shot made prior to taking up a position at the net.

Backhand   A shot played with the reverse side of the racket and with the back of the hand facing the ball.

Ball-boy (or girl)   In major championships, ball-boys (or girls) are employed to collect stray balls in between rallies so as not to interrupt the players' concentration. When playing on your local park, however, you do not have that luxury and have to take it in turns to go out of the court to find balls hit over the surrounding fence . . .

Ball in play   The ball is in play from the moment it is hit in the service. Unless a fault or let is called it remains in play until the point is decided.

Baseline   The line marking the end of the court is the baseline. There is one at each end.

Baseline play   When play takes place with the players hitting the ball to each other from near the baseline.

Centre line   The line that divides the service court into two halves. If the server is delivering to the service court on his left, he must stand to the right of the centre line, and vice versa. The receiver may stand wherever he sees fit, so long as he remains on his side of the net!

The cross-court drive

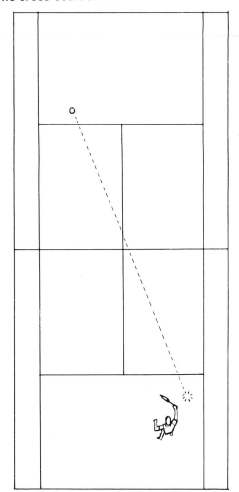

A shot played from one side of the court to the other is a cross-court drive.

Centre service line   The alternative, and more specific, name for the centre line.

Cross court shot   A shot played diagonally across the court.

Deep volley   A volley that lands close to your opponent's baseline.

TENNIS

The drop shot

A ball delicately played so that it falls to the ground just beyond the net is known as a drop shot.

Deuce   If each player wins three points then the score becomes deuce. The next point becomes 'advantage' to one player (see above). If the scores become level after the next rally, it returns to deuce, and so on.

Double fault   If you fail to make a proper serve with your two attempts it is a double fault and your opponent wins the point.

Doubles   A match involving two players per side. They can either be two players of the same sex (men's or women's doubles) or of the opposite sex (mixed doubles).

Drop shot   A shot played so that it drops just over the net. It is normally played with backspin to prevent it bouncing too high once it goes over the net.

Fault   A serve that either goes into the net or does not first land in the correct service court is a fault. If the next serve is also a fault then it is a double fault and the server loses the point.

Foot fault   A service that infringes the foot fault rules (see page 31) is a foot fault and is treated like an ordinary fault.

Forehand   A shot made with the front face of the racket and with the forearm facing the ball is a forehand shot.

Flat service   A service made by striking the ball with a flat racket face and thus not applying spin to the ball.

Game   A game lasts until one player has won four points, provided he has won at least two more than his opponent. If not, the game continues until he is two points clear, at which stage he wins the game.

Ground stroke   A shot played after the ball has bounced.

Half-volley   A stroke made at the same moment as the ball hits the ground is a half-volley.

In   A ball is said to be 'in' if any part of it lands within the confines of the court.

Let   As in most racket sports, in tennis the let is used to replay a point. If a player is interfered with by an outside source or a serve is made before the receiver is ready, then a let is called. However, in tennis the let also has another meaning.
   If the service hits the net cord and bounces into the correct service court, the point is replayed without penalty. However, if it hits the net and bounces OUT of the

service court or into the wrong service court then it is a fault. In major championships, a net cord judge sits close to the net to make a decision on whether it is a let or not.

Linesmen (or women) At major events linesmen (or women) assist the umpire in deciding whether a ball is in or out of court. The umpire can overrule a linesman's call if he thinks he (she) made the wrong call.

Lob A shot directed high into the air and into your opponent's half of the court.

Love If a player has not scored a point his score is 'love'.

Love game A game in which one player wins without his opponent scoring a point.

Playing a forehand shot.

Match A match consists of a pre-determined number of sets. Normally five in men's singles and men's doubles, and three for women's singles and doubles, and mixed doubles.

Match point If a player needs just one point to win the match he is said to have match point. If he leads 40-30 he has one match point. If the score is 40-15 he has two match points and if it is 40-love then he has three match points.

Scoring

This is how the scores might look at the end of a five-set match. Brown won by three sets to two – having been two sets down!

SET	1	2	3	4	5
J.SMITH	6	6	6	1	8
A. BROWN	4	3	7	6	10

The passing shot

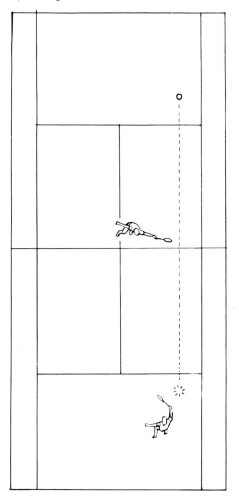

A winning passing shot.

Net game   When a player adopts a position close to the net and begins a volleying game he is said to be playing a 'net game'.

New balls   As we said earlier, new balls are normally introduced into major championships every nine games. It is up to the player serving with the new balls to indicate to the receiver, normally by holding the balls up, to show they are new.

Out   A ball is 'out' if no part of it lands within the confines of the court.

Passing shot   A shot which goes past your opponent while he or she is at the net is a passing shot.

Rally   A sequence of shots made by the players to each other is a rally.

Referee   The supreme official at any event or championship. He is responsible for the overall control of the event and has the power to overrule the umpire's decisions.

Seeding   Seeding is common to many sports these days, but lawn tennis has had seeding for more than sixty years. The idea of seeding is to make sure the best players remain in the competition as long as possible. Theoretically the number one and two seeds should contest every final, while the three and four seeds should make it to the semi-final stage, and so on. Happily, outsiders frequently come along and upset the seedings, otherwise tennis, and other sports that adopt seeding, would be pretty boring.

Service   The stroke that starts each point. The service must be made by hitting the ball into the opposite service court and it must bounce before being returned.

Set   A set consists of at least six games. The first person to win six games wins the set provided he is at least two games clear of his opponent. If not, the set continues until one player has the two-game advantage. If the tie-break is being used it comes into operation when the game gets to 6-all. Whoever wins the tie-break wins the set 7-6.

Set point   Same as match point, except this time it is when one player is on the verge of winning the set.

EQUIPMENT · & · TERMINOLOGY

Umpiring

The umpire sits in an elevated chair positioned level with the net. He has a clear view of all the play.

Singles sticks   If a court is fitted with one net for use in both singles and doubles matches a singles stick is placed in the ground 0.91m (3ft) from the sideline for a game of singles. It should support the net at a height of 1.07m (3ft 6in). The area of net between the singles stick and outer post is deemed to be a permanent fixture.

Smash   A ball hit above the head and powerfully into the opposing half of the court.

Stop volley   A volley, usually made close to the net, which forces the ball to drop into your opponent's half of the court and just over the net.

Tie-break   To prevent long sets the tie-break was introduced in 1970. If the number of games gets to 6-all then the tie-break is played. The first person to reach seven points, provided he is at least two points clear of his opponent, wins the tie-break and the set. The tie-break may not be used in the final set of a match.

Top spin   A deceptive shot with a lot of spin that causes the ball to dip sharply in flight.

Slice   A shot played with backspin and possibly side-spin.

Umpire   Unfortunately, when you play at your local park you will not have the luxury of an umpire. The honesty and integrity of the two players will be called upon to decide dubious decisions. (If you are ever in any doubt, simply play a let). However, in major championships the umpire sits on an elevated chair overlooking the net. He has control of play on the court and is responsible for keeping and confirming the score to the players.

The volley

To play a volley, you must strike the ball before it hits the ground.

Volley   A stroke made before the ball hits the ground. The receiver can volley at any time except from the service, when he must let the serve bounce in the service court first

The indomitable Jimmy Connors reaches to play a drop volley.

THE GAME –
A GUIDE

As with other racket sports, the object of tennis is to win rallies in order to score points. However, unlike some similar sports you do not have to be the server to win points in lawn tennis. You can win points as either the server or receiver.

The object of the game is simple: to hit the ball over the net and into your opponent's half of the court so that he is unable to return it over the net to you.

A match consists of a pre-determined number of sets up to a maximum of five for a match involving men and three involving women.

The tossing of a coin or a racket shall decide which player serves first. Both players are entitled to a warm-up, or practice, period at the commencement of a match, or re-start of an interrupted match. Whoever wins the toss can either choose whether he becomes the first server or receiver, in which case the other player has the choice of ends. Alternatively, the player winning the toss can have the choice of ends, thus giving the other player the choice of serving or receiving. The players stand on opposite sides of the net.

THE · SERVICE

Once the server has been established the first service starts the game. At the start of every new game the first service is always made from the server's right-hand side of the court and the ball must be hit over the net into the diagonally opposite service court.

At the time of making the service the server must stand with both feet behind the

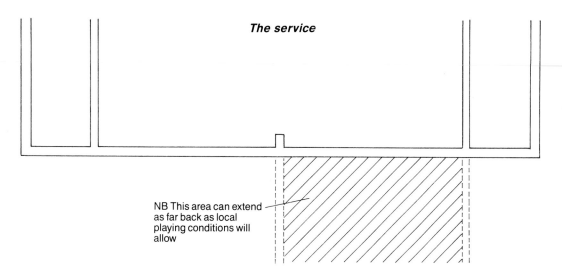

The service

If you are serving from the right-hand court your feet must be placed within the shaded area. (Vice versa from the left-hand court.)

NB This area can extend as far back as local playing conditions will allow

baseline and between the imaginary extensions of the centre mark and sideline (not the extreme sideline, but the one indicating the extent of the singles court).

To make a legal and successful serve, the ball should be thrown into the air with the hand NOT holding the racket and, before it hits the ground, be hit by the racket. The service is deemed to be made the moment the racket makes contact with the ball. For the service to be good it must land in the diagonally opposite service court. If it does not the server has a second chance to make a good serve.

If the serve is not good, a fault is called and he has another attempt at making a good service. If that should also be a fault then a double fault is called and a point goes to the opposing player. The next point starts with the server standing on the opposite side of the baseline (i.e. to the left of the centre mark). After every point has been played, the service alternates from one side of the centre mark to the other.

If, after a serve, the ball is returned by the receiver, then the rally continues until one player fails to return the ball or the ball is played into the net or out of the court. Once the rally is over, the next serve takes place and, as already said, from the opposite side of the centre mark.

Foot fault

A server will be foot-faulted if either foot touches any area other than that behind the baseline and within the imaginary extension of the centre mark and sideline. However, it is also a foot fault if a server changes his position by walking or running into the serve. A foot fault is treated like a normal fault.

Changing ends

Players change ends at the completion of the first, third and subsequent alternate games in each set. If the set ends on an odd number, say 6-3, the players change ends. They next change ends after the first game of the next set. However, if the set ends 6-4 then they do not change at the end of the set. They do, however, change after the first

Foot fault

game of the following set. A rest period lasting a maximum ninety seconds is allowed while players change ends.

WINNING · & · LOSING · POINTS

There are several ways in which points can be won or lost. The following are the most common ways.

At the service, the server wins the point if the ball hits the receiver, or any part of his clothing or his racket, before it hits the ground. If the receiver fails to return the ball over the net after it has landed in the correct service court the server wins the point.

The receiver automatically wins the point if the server double faults. At other times you will lose points if:

(a) You allow the ball in play to bounce twice before successfully returning it over the net.

(b) You return a ball and it does not cross the net.

(c) You return a ball over the net but it bounces outside your opponent's half of the court. The ball is then said to be 'out'.

(d) You hit the ball more than once in one stroke.

(e) You volley the ball before it crosses the net.

(f) You, or anything you wear, or your racket, touches the net, net cord, net supporting posts or ground within your opponent's part of the court.

(g) You throw your racket at the ball . . . if you throw it at anything, or anybody else,

It is a foot fault if any part of the foot touches the baseline at the moment the racket makes contact with the ball.

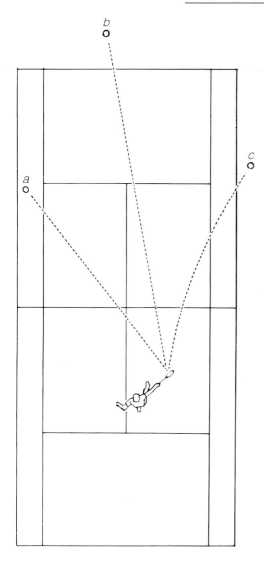

Ball hit out

The shots illustrated here (a, b, c) are all 'out'. However, 'a' would be 'in' if you were playing doubles.

Volleying on the wrong side of the net

You are not allowed to volley the ball until it has crossed the net into your half of the court.

you can expect an even more severe penalty!

(h) The ball touches you or any of your clothing, other than your racket.

Umpires these days are concerned about the increasing amount of misconduct on court and they have the power to award conduct violation points against a player for any action that they feel is not within the spirit of the game. Persistently breaking the rules can

cost you the match. **You have been warned.**

In addition to the above, you will also lose the point if it is deemed that you have deliberately hindered your opponent in making a stroke.

Ball in or out

A ball is deemed to be in the court if **any part of it** hits the sideline or baseline. The same

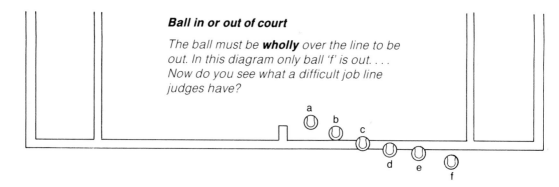

Ball in or out of court

*The ball must be **wholly** over the line to be out. In this diagram only ball 'f' is out. . . . Now do you see what a difficult job line judges have?*

applies if the ball hits the service or centre service line at the service.

Now for the important part . . .

SCORING

Scoring in tennis is simple, not that you would think so when you listen to some players!

The first point won by a player is called 15; the second is 30; and the third 40. The next point is game. A player can only win a game when he is two points clear of his opponent. So, if the score gets to 40–30, the player on 40 will win the game if he wins the next point. However, if he loses the next point the score goes to 'deuce' and the game continues until one player has a two-point advantage.

To clarify the scoring even further, let us assume two players (A and B) are taking part in a singles match. This is how the scoring would go:

Point	Score	
won by	A	B
A	15	love
A	30	love
B	30	15
A	40	15
B	40	30
B	Deuce	
A	Advantage A	
B	Deuce	
B	Advantage B	
B	Game B	

What could be simpler?

The set scoring has already been outlined in the Terminology section on page 26. However, we ought to explain further about the tie-breaker.

Tie-break

Not all competitions use the tie-break, and it is not compulsory, but most major championships have been using it since the early 1970s.

Numerical scoring (1, 2, 3, etc.) as opposed to conventional tennis scoring (15, 30, 40) is used throughout the tie-break. The person who should be serving next, if the match was continuing normally, serves first in the tie-break. He only serves for the first point, after which the service passes to the other player. He then serves for two

John McEnroe of the USA, a player of exceptional ability with an equally exceptional temperament!

points and the players then take it in turns to serve for two points alternately until a winner has been found.

The first player to reach seven points wins the tie-break and thus wins the set 7-6. However, like most aspects of tennis, you have to be two points clear of your opponent before you win the tie-break. You cannot win it 7-6, 8-7, 9-8 etc. It must be 7-5, 8-6, 9-7 and so on.

Players change ends at the completion of every six points and also at the end of the tie-break game.

The player who served first in the tie-break game shall *receive* service in the first game of the next set.

THE · OFFICIALS

In practice the majority of matches are played without any official. It is up to the players to be honest with each other (and themselves) and make decisions that will affect the game. However, at club level, an umpire will officiate over any match which is a league game or similar. At international and major championship level the umpire will be assisted by judges.

Unless a referee is appointed, the umpire is the sole arbitrator. However, if there is a referee, appeals can be made to him, and he has the power to overrule any decisions made by the umpire.

If an umpire receives assistance from judges they will be positioned as shown in the diagram and their task is to make decisions on points of fact i.e. if a ball was in or out, or whether the service was a foot fault, or whether the ball was a let. If judges

If the umpire receives the assistance of judges, this is where they sit. All major championship matches are adjudicated by this many officials. Some top tournaments use an 'electronic eye' on the service line to help with decisions about the service.

Judges' positions

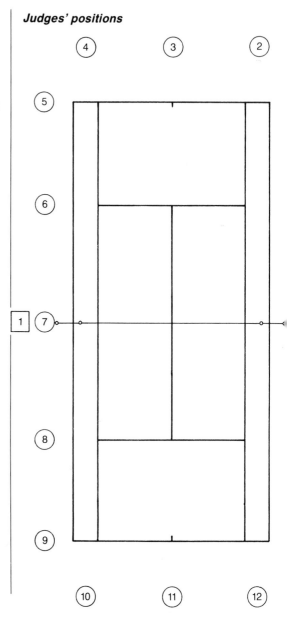

1 = the umpire   6 and 8 = service line judges   3 and 11 are centre service line judges   7 = the net cord judge.   All other judges rule whether balls are in or out, and assist with foot fault decisions.

Serving in doubles

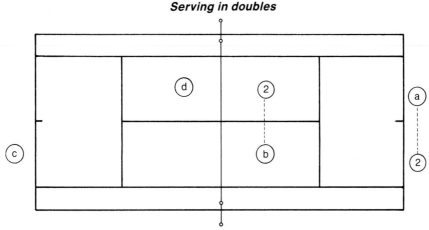

'a' and 'b' are playing together, and 'c' and 'd' form the other pair. In the first game, 'a' serves to 'c' for the first service. At the start of the second point he serves to 'd', but from position 2. 'b' also moves to his position 2. At the end of the game 'c' serves next to either 'a' or 'b', then in the third game 'b' serves, starting with 'c'. Finally, in the fourth service game, 'd' serves to either 'a' or 'b', who shall be the same player who first received the service from 'c' at the beginning of the match. And so it continues, in the same order.

are not in a position to make such a decision they should indicate accordingly to the umpire who should take on the task himself. If he cannot make a decision, he has the power to call a let.

DOUBLES · PLAY

The first thing to remember about doubles play is that the court area is larger by virtue of the fact that the tramlines come into play making the playing area 9ft (2.74m) wider.

The service is the same in doubles play as in singles and must be made to the diagonal service box. However, the order of service must be decided at the beginning of each set and adhered to throughout that set.

If you serve in game 1 then your partner will serve in game 3. Game 2 is served by one of your opponents while game 4 is served by the other member of the opposing side. That

order must be retained throughout the set. It can be changed at the commencement of the next set.

The team who are the receivers in the first game decides which player shall receive the first service. That player then receives the first service in every odd-numbered game throughout the set. The other team, when they become receivers, make the same choice, and that player receives the first service in every even-numbered game throughout the set.

The server will, as in singles, start the game by serving from the right-hand side of the court, and alternately after each point. The receiving players do not change sides after each point, they retain their positions and take it in turn to become a receiver.

Once the serve has been returned the rally continues and either player from one side can play the ball; they do not have to play alternate shots as in table tennis.

If a service hits the server's partner then it is a fault. If it hits the receiver's partner before the ball hits the ground the serving team win the point.

If the **tie-break** is introduced into a doubles game then the player who is scheduled to serve next serves the first point. Thereafter the service alternates as in the singles game but in accordance with the order already played within the set. The pair who serve first in the tie-break game will receive the first service in the opening game of the next set.

RULES CLINIC

What happens if a service is made from the wrong half of the court?

All play resulting from the service will stand, but the moment the error is spotted the correct serving point should be taken up before the next service.

If I notice my opponent served from the wrong half of the court on his first service and it was a fault, does he have to complete the service from that half of the court or should he move to the correct half immediately?

He should move to the correct half of the court immediately, but has only one service left on that point.

If my opponent serves and then I realize it is my turn to serve what happens?

The fault should be rectified immediately, but all points scored before the error was noticed shall count. However, if the error is noted after your opponent has served a fault, the fault does not carry over to you when you become the server.

What about doubles? Surely it must happen often that the wrong player serves? What happens then?

Well, it doesn't happen at the top level, but it does happen in the local park. Once the error is discovered the correct sequence should be reverted to and all points scored during the error shall count. The same applies if the receivers take the service in the wrong order.

If players go to the wrong ends after changing service when should the error be rectified?

As soon as it is noticed. All points scored up to that time shall count however.

During an indoor game, the ball from a service hits a rafter and then bounces into the correct service court. Is the service good or not?

It would be a fault. Any ball that hits a permanent fixture from the service is a fault. Permanent fixtures include such things as stands, permanent seating and their occupants . . . which could well be a judge!

TENNIS

If the server throws the ball up and then fails to hit it, is it a fault?

Yes. Just like in golf, it is a 'fresh air' shot, and counts.

. . . but if the server decides to abort the serve after throwing the ball up, is it still a fault?

No.

If you throw the ball up to serve, swing at it and miss, it is a fault.

Is a let called if the ball hits the top of the net and goes into the correct court during a normal rally?

No. If can only be called a let at the service.

Can I catch the ball on my racket?

Yes, you most probably can. But if you do the point goes to your opponent!

What happens if a ball becomes damaged during a rally?

A let should be called and the point should be replayed.

If I play a shot then deliberately hit my racket on to the ground and distort the shape of it before returning the ball for a winning shot do I still get the point?

No. You are not allowed to deliberately and materially change the shape of your racket during the playing of a point. Mind you, if you have time to damage your racket, and *then* play a winning shot you must be some player . . .

What happens if my racket becomes damaged during a rally?

You will have to wait until the end of the point to change it.

If I play a shot that hits the ground within the confines of the court and then hits the stop-netting at the back of the court before my opponent can reach it, is it a winning point?

Yes. The same applies if the ball hits any other permanent fixture, provided you hit a good ball into the opposing court first.

If I return a ball and it hits the net post and then goes into the opposing court, does it count or is a let called?

It counts as a legitimate point.

You said earlier that I cannot lean over the net to volley a ball in the other half of the court. But what would happen if my opponent played a shot, it bounced in my half of the court and then the wind took it back over to his side of the net?

You would be allowed to play the ball provided you did not touch the net with your body, clothing or racket.

What happens if my racket accidentally slips out of my hand and hits the net, do I lose the point?

Yes, provided the ball is in play at the time. Mind you, you were warned to take some talcum powder on to the court with you weren't you . . ?

TENNIS

Does a player have to be standing in the court to make a shot?

No. He can be anywhere, except in his opponent's area of the court.

If I play a volley close to the net, hit the ball in my half of the court, but then allow my racket to follow-through and go over the net, am I penalized?

No, but again you must make sure you don't touch the net.

Playing a shot – where from?

Providing you stay on your side of the net, and so long as there is enough room to move freely around the perimeters of the court, you may play a shot from wherever you like.

Does a ball that hits another ball lying on the court have to be played as a let?

No, the shot counts. Mind you, if it happened at Wimbledon the umpire would certainly have a few choice words to say to the ball-boy (or girl)!

If I am hindered from playing my shot is a let called?

Yes, unless you are hindered by a permanent fixture. Let's say a pigeon flies across your sight just as you're about to play, that is certainly outside interference, and a pigeon could not be described as a permanent fixture . . .

You keep mentioning 'permanent fixtures' . . . what exactly are they?

The laws of the game describe a permanent fixture thus: 'The net, posts, singles sticks, cord or metal cables, strap and band. Also, where there are any; the back and side stops, the stands, fixed or movable seats and chairs around the court, and their occupants, all other fixtures above and around the court, and the umpire, net-cord judge, foot-fault judge, linesmen and ball-boys (or girls) when in their respective places.'

Can the server's feet be off the ground at the time of the service?

Yes, but at the moment of striking the ball his foot (or feet) must not touch the baseline or court the other side of the baseline.

Feet off the ground at service

*It is perfectly legal to have both feet off the ground while serving. Your feet must not touch the baseline or the court beyond it. However, your feet can be over the baseline at the point of service as long as they remain in the air – it is just that they must not touch the court until **after** racket and ball have made contact.*

returning the ball is considerably harder. How close you stand to the net depends on the strength of your opponent's serve.

How is the 1½ minute break in between games timed?

The time is taken from the moment the ball goes out of play at the end of the game to the time the ball is struck for the first point of the next game.

Is there a time limit on the amount of time a server can take in between the end of one point and serving to start the next?

In major international events this is normally 30 seconds.

How often are the balls changed during the tie-break game?

Not at all. The tie-break game is counted as one game for the purpose of the ball change. If the balls, however, are due to be changed at the beginning of the tie-break, the change is delayed until it is completed.

Where does the receiver have to stand when taking the service?

Anywhere, provided it is in his own half of the court. Understandably, it makes sense to stand in the half of the court to where the server is serving otherwise the job of

The young West German star, Steffi Graf, a player of immense power and the main pretender to Martina Navratilova's long-held crown.

TECHNIQUE

Now that the theory is over it is down to a bit of practical work . . . learning the techniques of the game.

The starting place must be with the racket. If you cannot hold the racket properly then you have got problems right from the start. So let's start with the grip.

THE · GRIP

It is important to realize that you need to adopt a different grip when playing different strokes.

The most common grip, and the one used for the forehand drive, which will cater for the majority of your shots, is what is called the **eastern forehand**.

It is also known as the 'shake hands' grip because you grip the handle as if you were shaking hands with it. To make sure you adopt the perfect grip hold the racket in your left hand; place the palm of your right hand on the strings and slide it down the racket, keeping the palm in the same position, until you reach the handle. Now wrap your fingers around the handle . . . shake hands with it if you like. You should now have complete control of the racket for playing those forehand shots.

Don't have your fingers too tense, and don't have them too close together. Your first finger should be in a position that looks as though it is going to pull the trigger of a gun.

A good solid grip will prevent any 'wristy' action. The racket is an extension of your

Forehand grip

TECHNIQUE

Backhand grip

The basic backhand grip. Note how the hand is moved anti-clockwise around the handle and the thumb is tucked under the handle for extra support.

Spread the fingers

Make sure your fingers are not too close together. Note the first finger – doesn't it look as though it is going to pull the trigger of a gun?

arm and a firm wrist is a must.

A grip developed for use on concrete surfaces is the **western forehand.** It is ideal for those balls which bounce that bit higher. Unlike the eastern forehand, the thumb is moved clockwise on to the top of the handle. Because the palm of the hand is 'under' the handle, it makes the playing of low shots that bit more difficult, but it is ideal for shots waist-high and above.

A popular grip among less experienced players is the **semi-western forehand**, whereby the thumb is moved back towards its eastern position. As a newcomer, you are well advised to adopt the semi-western grip, before you try to master the full western.

The next grip we will look at is for the **backhand** drive.

Many inexperienced players have a difficult time playing the backhand. But this inability to play the shot – or should we call it *fear* – stems from the fact that a poor grip is adopted. The main cause of this is the difficulty most novices have in changing their grip from the eastern forehand to the backhand during a rally. But remember, **you will have extreme difficulty playing a successful backhand shot with an eastern forehand grip.**

To change your grip into a backhand grip you should adopt the eastern forehand, but move your hand anti-clockwise around the handle so that your thumb nicely tucks underneath and the palm of your hand is now more on top of the handle. The effect of wrapping the thumb around the handle is to put the firmness into the grip and stroke.

It is important to make sure the fingers are not too close together again, otherwise the grip will be too wristy. It is important with the backhand shot to make sure the wrist is locked solid onto the handle.

A common fault with novices when playing the backhand is to play the shot with slice i.e. the racket slides under the ball and imparts spin. The racket head should be played through the ball with an open face. There are times when you will want to play the backhand with slice, but that is a specialist shot, and not one that you should be playing just yet.

Many players adopt the two-handed grip for the backhand. The same grip as above is adopted but the other hand is placed adjacent to the gripping hand to give extra support and power.

The biggest problem you will encounter initially is the ability to change grips fast enough during an actual rally. But don't worry, it will come in time and you will soon be able to change without thinking about it.

Simply because you lack the confidence to play the backhand, don't rely on the forehand for all your shots. This is fatal, and will cost you many points. It would most probably pay you to tackle the problem in the opposite way – get yourself in a position to play the backhand at every stroke. That way you will find it much easier to switch grips for the forehand shot.

I cannot stress enough at this stage that you should practise the backhand shot. There is no sense in being good at the forehand without being able to introduce other shots into your repertoire.

Those two grips are for the game's two fundamental shots. But there are more . . . For **serving** and playing the **overhead smash** you are well advised to adopt the eastern forehand grip and play the shot with an open racket face. You will soon realize, once you have mastered the simple serve, that you want to serve or smash with spin on the ball. It is only when you feel confident that you start serving or smashing with an advanced grip that looks more like the backhand drive grip.

For playing the **forehand or backhand volley** you should adopt the same grips as for your normal forehand and backhand drives. When you gain more experience and confidence you will find yourself adopting the **advanced service grip**. This will enable you, after serving, to progress to the net to

Two-handed backhand

Note how the normally redundant left hand adds support and power to the racket as this right-handed player plays a backhand.

play a volley without having to change your grip. But we will look at all that a little bit later.

Finally, whereabouts should you grip the handle? Answer: as near as possible to the end. That way you will get the maximum effect of the racket. If you have to grip the handle nearer to the head because it is too heavy then you are well advised to get yourself another racket.

There are five fundamentals you should always bear in mind: (1) keep your eye on the ball (2) have good balance and footwork (3) make sure you have a good swing (4) control the racket movement and (5) control the racket face.

You should always **keep your eye on the ball.** You must keep your eye on that ball right up to the moment it makes contact with your racket. Get into the habit of doing that right from the start. If you don't you will be leaving a lot of your shots to chance.

Getting quickly around the court is important, but it is no use getting into the right position if you are off balance. Think what you are doing with your feet all the time, because good footwork helps create **good balance.**

Having got into position and balanced your body correctly, you should have no problem in employing a **good swing.** Both the backswing and follow-through should be fluent. Provided your balance and footwork are right then you should have little difficulty in perfecting a good swing.

However, if there are some flaws in your footwork then **controlling the racket movement** is going to prove difficult. You must have complete control over the racket.

Don't expect it to do all the work. It is like a computer, it will only do what the operator tells it to!

Controlling the racket face is as important as any of the other fundamentals, because if you cannot control the face then you are not likely to play any winning shots. Racket face control comes down to the right grip for the right shot. Keep the grip firm and imagine the racket as an extension to your arm.

PLAYING · THE · DIFFERENT · SHOTS

Right, you know how to hold the racket for the different shots. It is time we taught you how to play the shots:

Firstly, the shot that starts off each point, the **Service**.

If you watch the top players you will be astounded at the pace they put into the service stroke, and with consistent accuracy. However, whatever you do, don't try and emulate the likes of Ivan Lendl, John McEnroe or Boris Becker the first time you try to serve. Don't run before you can walk. Experience will tell you when you are ready to start experimenting with a more powerful serve and one with spin.

However, we will look at the basics. Incidentally, the following assumes that you are right-handed.

You take up position with a sideways stance. Your left foot should point towards the right-hand net post. The feet should be 38–45cm (15–18in) apart. The racket head should be pointing towards the service court you intend serving to. Your two hands should be in contact with the racket but as you drop your racket ready to go into the backswing, your left hand (the one holding

the ball) swings into an upright position. It then releases the ball upwards. Many novices make the mistake of releasing the ball too early and it is thrown at an angle and towards the net rather than upwards – consequently you have to stretch to play the shot. The correct position of the ball at the moment of impact should be about 30cm (1ft) in front of the left foot. The ball should be thrown to a height of about 45cm (18in) above your normal reach.

While the ball is on its way upwards, the racket should start its 'throwing' movement into the ball. Your bodyweight is now starting to switch from your back foot to your front foot. Your left arm, which is now redundant, starts to swing forward thus helping the pendulum movement of your entire body. At the top of the reach the racket arm should be perfectly straight and you should reach as far as possible to hit the ball. The head of the racket should be 'thrown' in an 'up-and-over' action and should hit the falling ball accurately. If you don't keep your eyes on the ball there is little chance of you making a good service.

After making contact with the ball you should follow through, and the momentum

Gabriela Sabatini of Argentina, about to serve at Wimbledon, 1987.

THE · SERVICE

Throw the ball up . . .

*Ball going up,
racket going back.*

*Left foot pointing
towards net post,
racket pointing towards
service court.*

. . . and contact at top of reach.

Eye on ball . . .

Finally, the follow through.

The forehand drive

Left: *The 'ready' position.*

Below: *Feet nicely in position, knees slightly bent.*

of the swing will carry you forward and into the court ready to meet any return. Some players like to get close to the net as soon as possible after making the service but, like all aspects of the game, that comes with confidence and experience.

The most common error in serving is in the placing of the ball. You will at first find a lack of consistency in this respect. You are well advised in your early days of development to concentrate on getting the placement right and just making sure the ball goes into the correct service court. At this stage, the

service will have little impact on the outcome of the game, so just concentrate on developing a simple but effective service. Getting the co-ordination between left and right hand is more important than anything. Once you have that sorted out then serving will become second nature.

When you are ready to develop on to the advanced serve applied with spin, then you need to adopt the advanced grip as outlined on page 49. It is more like the backhand grip than the forehand, consequently, as you play the shot you will more easily impart spin

Shot played sideways on and not too close to the body.

. . . and the follow through.

on the ball.

Once you have mastered the serve you need to experiment by trying to place the ball into one half or the other of the service court, thus confusing your opponent. If you know he is weak on his backhand, then you should regularly serve to his backhand.

That's the service out of the way. But what happens if your opponent returns it . . . you have got to know what shot to play, and how to play it.

Let's start with the **forehand drive.**

The forehand drive is the most widely used shot in a game of tennis. It is also the easiest to play. Because of this, many inexperienced players rely on the shot too much and rather than adopt a position to play the backhand, will get in position, albeit the wrong one, to play the forehand. However, you will use it a lot, so let's see how to play it.

Once you can see the ball is coming to your forehand make sure you have the correct grip (you won't have time to look at your grip, but you will be able to tell by the feel). When you play the forehand shot, the ball will be to your right so you have to make sure your feet are in the correct position. If you leave it too late to get into position you will be in awful trouble and will have to play the ball hurriedly and too close to your body. The result will be either a losing shot or a poor return.

I know you will not have a lot of time to get everything right, and it will take many hours of practice before these steps become instinctive. But you need to have your weight forward on the balls of your feet at the 'ready' position. The racket head should be approximately waist-high and the left hand should support the racket just below the head.

As you pivot to play the shot the body weight should be on the back foot. The wrist should be kept firm, and as you take the racket into the backswing the left arm can be outstretched to help with your balance. As the shot is made, the weight is transferred to the front foot with a step forward. The racket should make contact with the ball at full arm's length and should be rising as it hits the ball. Again, keep your eyes on the ball up to the point of impact – this cannot be stressed enough. After completing the shot the racket should follow through and you should quickly get into position for your next shot . . . unless you have played a winning shot of course!

Of course, playing deceptive shots is all

part of the game, and the forehand lends itself to greater scope in the playing of such shots. The forehand shot can be hit with topspin, underspin or flat (with no spin at all). Of course, where you hit the ball determines where it is going to land on the other side of the net. You have to quickly assess your opponent's position and decide whether you are going to play a powerful passing drive or a cross-court shot. Only a specific game situation will dictate this decision.

Now for the **backhand**.
This shot petrifies new players but if you can get it into your head that it is just as easy to play as the forehand then you should have no problems. (It *isn't* as easy as the forehand, but get it into your head that it *is* and life will be a lot easier!)

As you move into position, your weight goes on to the back foot and the turning of the body into a sideways position starts on that foot. The racket head is again held approximately waist high, and is once more supported by the left hand.

When the racket moves into the backswing position, all your body weight is on the back foot and your right foot steps forward ready for you to play the ball from a sideways hitting position. The shot is played with a lot of movement of the shoulders, which rotate 90° into the shot. At the same time the weight is transferred to the front foot. The shot is made with the ball approximately level with the front knee, and is hit in an upward motion.

The most important thing to remember when playing the backhand drive is *keep that wrist firm*. If you don't, you will just 'kill' the ball when it hits the racket and the ball will most probably end up in the net . . .

Total concentration: American Chris Evert shows one of many qualities which have made her perhaps the most consistent and durable players of recent years.

The backhand drive

When playing the **double-handed backhand**, grip the racket with the left hand slightly above the right. Both wrists should be kept firm. Footwork is the same as in the single-handed backhand but balance is slightly more difficult to control. You will either need to take an extra step with your back foot after making the shot, or alternatively, take your supporting hand away from the racket as soon as the shot has been made.

The double-handed backhand gives you more power and control, but you have to be quick-thinking to get your hands in position to make the shot.

Both the forehand and backhand drives are played after the ball has hit the ground.

But there will be times when you see your partner out of position and rather than give him time to recover will want to play your shot on the volley i.e. before it hits the ground. You can play volleys either with the forehand or backhand. Let's have a look at both, starting with the **forehand volley**.

Like the forehand and backhand drives you should be in a 'ready' position facing the net. But when you play the shot it is from a sideways position. You pivot on your back foot, and hold your left arm out straight, to help your balance. This time the racket head is held considerably higher, and level with *your* head at the approach. As the racket is brought down you start to transfer the weight to your front foot as you 'walk' into the shot. As the ball approaches, your shoulders should be turned facing the net. The shot is played with a 'punching' motion and with a very firm wrist action. A long backswing is *not* needed for playing this shot. You are not applying any speed into the ball, but are using its own oncoming speed for the return volley.

The **half-volley** is a shot played immediately after the ball has bounced. Because of that, the ball is always hit close to the ground but the important thing to remember when playing the half-volley shot is to keep your back straight but allow the knees to bend. The back knee should be almost touching the ground. Provided you can get in position fast enough, you should

Above, left to right: *Keep your eye on the ball as it approaches, and move into position. Move your weight onto your back foot. Now step forward with the right, and transfer your weight to that foot. Play the shot with a firm wrist and keep the face of the racket 'open'. Finally, don't forget that flowing follow through!*

The double-handed backhand drive (releasing racket)

This shot is basically the same as the normal backhand shot. However, note how the left hand is removed from the handle as soon as the shot has been played.

There is a second method, where both hands stay in contact with the racket for the complete stroke.

play the shot from the side, but whatever, you must keep your eye on the ball and *keep that wrist firm.*

The reason for playing the half-volley is normally that you are in trouble and cannot play another shot. But you are well advised to learn how to play it, ready for the day when you will need it.

The **backhand volley** should, like the forehand volley, be played from a position about 3.05m (10ft) from the net for maximum

efficiency and control.

You should once again adopt a 'ready' position by facing the net and then pivot your body on your back foot. Make sure you have adopted the backhand grip and support the racket with your left hand. The backswing is very short and when the ball is played it should be well forward of the body. But this time the front foot will be forward to take the bodyweight. The shot is played with a short 'punching' action.

The biggest error in playing the backhand

volley is in allowing the wrist to slacken . . . I won't go on about keeping the wrist firm anymore, you know all about that by now don't you?

The backhand volley is a difficult stroke to play, and one which requires a lot of confidence. Inexperienced players often have trouble with this shot because they lack confidence. So: think positive; be positive!

The **backhand half-volley** is the same as the forehand half-volley (except that it is played with the backhand!) and the

important things to remember are the firm wrist (oh no! Not again . . .) and to bend the knees while keeping the back straight.

The forehand volley

Note how high the racket head is in the 'ready' position. You don't need a big backswing because you are only 'punching' the ball over the net. The shoulders should be square to the net at the moment of contact.

Stefan Edberg plays a
cross-court backhand

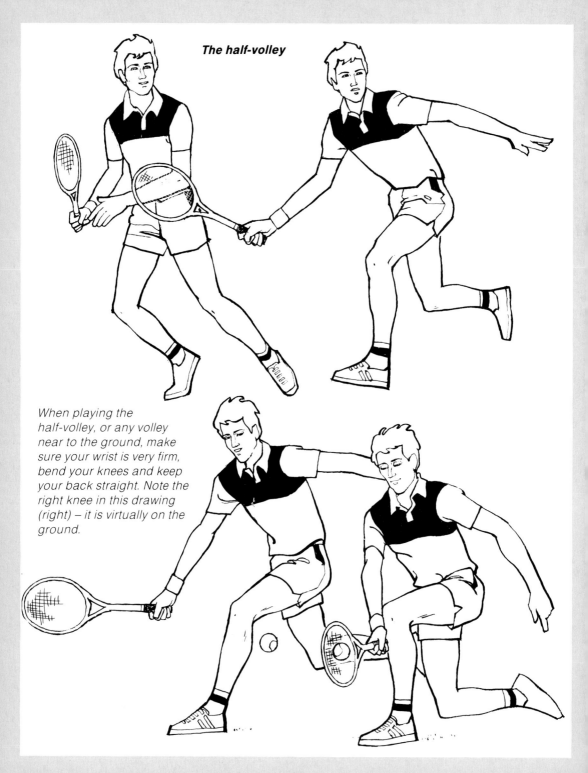

The half-volley

When playing the half-volley, or any volley near to the ground, make sure your wrist is very firm, bend your knees and keep your back straight. Note the right knee in this drawing (right) – it is virtually on the ground.

The backhand volley

The 'ready' position.
The left hand
supports the racket.

As you step onto your
right foot, support
your racket with the
left hand.

The shot is played
with a 'punching'
action, and contact
with the ball should
be just in front of the
right knee.

Let's now look at the **smash**.

An effective and powerful shot that is often a point winner. However, the biggest fault in playing the smash is taking your eye off the ball and rushing the shot. Once a novice sees the opportunity of the smash, the tendency is to get it over and done with as soon as possible. But that is a fatal error. Like any other shot, the preparation is important. After all, why should you rush just because it is likely to be a winning shot? You have a big advantage in playing the smash so don't mess it up by rushing things.

The smash should be used to counteract a lob from your opponent that has been hit short. The ideal position for the smash is again about 3.05m (10ft) from the net. It should be played from a sideways-on position. The smash is similar to the service and calls for perfect timing.

Having moved into a sideways position the free hand should be pointing out to the right. The shot should be made with full reach for maximum efficiency and, like the service, the racket should be 'thrown' through the ball. As you take the racket back behind your head you should transfer your weight from your front to your back foot and, as you stretch into the shot, your left hand should come round and face the ball.

As you start to 'throw' the racket into the

The smash

The smash demands a lot of different skills. Timing is the most important of these, but you must also keep your eye firmly on the ball, must hit the ball at the very top of your reach, and then 'throw' the racket through the ball.

ball the shoulders should move square to the net thus allowing maximum power and the shot should be made in a downwards motion on to the ball.

It is also possible to make a backhand smash, but I don't think we will go into that at this stage of your development. It is one of the most difficult shots to play and you needn't consider playing it until you are ready for your Centre Court debut at Wimbledon . . .

TENNIS

The lob

There are two forms of lob – the attacking lob and the defensive lob. The attacking lob (above) is likely to be a winning shot whereas the defensive version of the shot (top) is used to create time for movement into a better position on the court.

When lobbed defensively, the ball is hit with a great deal of underspin in a high trajectory. At impact the racket face should be kept wide open and the follow through should be high and long.

TECHNIQUE

When playing the attacking lob the face of the racket is lifted in an upwards movement to impart a lot of topspin on the ball.

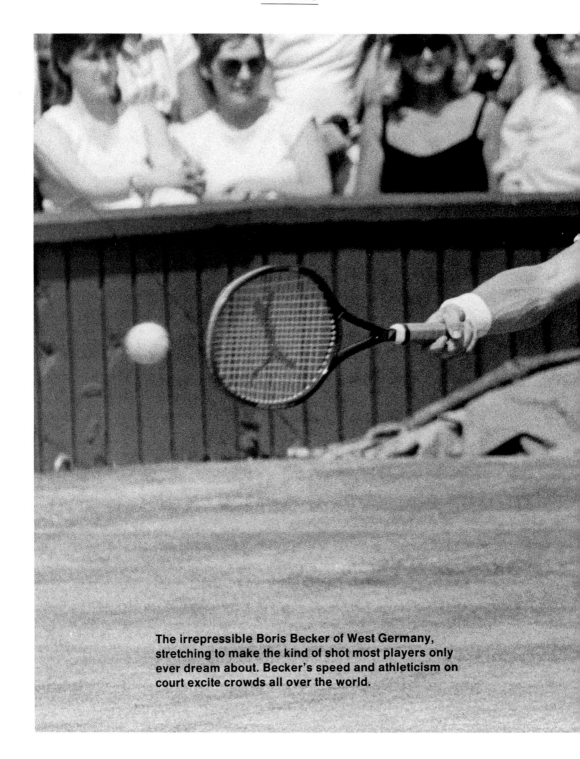

The irrepressible Boris Becker of West Germany, stretching to make the kind of shot most players only ever dream about. Becker's speed and athleticism on court excite crowds all over the world.

TENNIS

The drop shot

The key to the successful drop shot is to have the racket face open in order to impart the underspin necessary to 'check' the ball's movement once it lands on the other side of the net.

Finally let's have a look at the **lob** and the **drop shot**.

The lob is played either on the forehand or backhand but with an upward movement of the racket, the effect of which is to make the ball travel in an arc. The purpose of the lob is to play a shot over your opponent and out of his reach. Obviously, the nearer he is to the net the more chance there is of you effectively playing the lob.

The drop shot is a disguised shot that just drops over the net into your opponent's half of the court. When playing it, either on the forehand or backhand, the racket face needs to be open in both cases so as to impart underspin on the ball and cause it not to bounce too much when it lands. In making both shots, a good backswing, firm wrist, and 'eyes on the ball' are most important.

Summarizing: when playing the backhand or forehand drive the racket should be SWUNG through the ball; when playing the smash or serving the racket should be THROWN through the ball; and when playing the volley the racket should be PUNCHED through the ball.

Let's now have a look at the effects of spin.

Once you have mastered the basic shots as already outlined you can then experiment by putting spin on the ball. Furthermore you will be able to understand what happens to a ball that has spin put on it by your opponent.

There are three basic types of spin which you can put on the ball; topspin, underspin, and sidespin. You can also play shots with intermediate spin between topspin and sidespin.

A ball played with topspin will dip while in flight and it will bounce higher than normal after hitting the ground. A ball hit with underspin flattens the trajectory and will 'deaden' the bounce on landing. Sidespin will cause the ball to spin away to the right or left (depending on which side you impart the spin) while in flight and upon making contact with the ground. Don't forget, if you try to volley a ball with spin on it then it may leave your racket at an 'unusual' trajectory.

Topspin is commonly used with the forehand drive when you can apply both power and spin to the ball and thus making it an effective shot if played correctly. To play the forehand drive with topspin the racket should be swung on an upward path and with the racket face open and lifted as it makes contact with the ball.

To play a shot with underspin the racket face has to be open and the racket head played down through the ball at an angle. Sidespin is played similarly but the racket

head is played through the ball at an angle and along the side of the ball.

Both topspin and sidespin are useful in the service. A slower service with a lot of sidespin can cause your opponent as much trouble as a flat-hit fast service.

The secret of being able to cope with spin played against you is being able to read your opponent's next shot. It is not easy to disguise spin and you should keep your eye on the ball. If you do that correctly you will follow the path of your opponent's racket and the flight of the ball. If you correctly read your opponent's shot you can get in position to return it without any problems, whether it has spin on it or not, and make a successful return by imparting your own spin on the ball.

What about some **tactics?**

Knowing where to stand within the court is important. At the service you should stand near the baseline, depending on the amount of power your opponent puts into his first

Spin

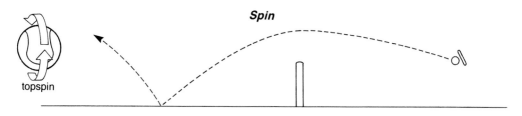

The effect of topspin and subsequent bounce of the ball.

Note the low bounce of the ball played with underspin.

A ball played with sidespin (on the right-hand side of the ball), will deflect like this after bouncing in the opposite court.

serve. If the first serve is a fault then you should move closer to the service line, but not too close, for the second serve.

After making the return, ideally you should return to a position near the centre of the court to cover any contingencies. But you mustn't be too near the baseline. Play will be dictated normally by one player taking up a position at the net and playing the volleying game. In this case you need to stand further back in your court and attempt to make the return by playing a lob which will take him off guard and force him back into the court and away from the net.

As a novice you will be happy just to get the ball over the net and make a rally. But once you become more adept you will want to try and outwit your opponent. *Brains as well as brawn help win tennis matches.*

You will want to vary your shots. Play some with topspin, some with sidespin, and even vary where you place them. If you place one shot deep into your opponent's court to his backhand and can play his return immediately into the opposite corner then he has to make up some ground to reach the shot . . . he'll soon get tired if you can constantly play a range of shots like that. But don't forget – he can always do the same to you!

Tennis at senior level is a power game these days. The server will often put a powerful first service in and, after hitting the return of serve, will take up a position at the net ready to play a winning shot. But what happens if the receiver returns that shot . . . then different tactics have to be employed.

The power game is not good enough alone to win matches: you must be able to play those deceptive cross-court shots, deep or angled shots, drop shots, and so on. This is when tennis becomes a tactical game – one player trying to outwit, as well as out-power, the other.

Before you can employ any tactics you must make sure you keep the ball in play. It may sound obvious, but often a novice will concentrate too hard on playing the 'difficult' shot, when the easy one will suffice. Try and keep your opponent behind the baseline – you have more chance of winning if you do. Don't forget, you do not have to play a winning shot to win a rally; most rallies are won through your opponent playing a 'losing' shot.

It is important that you maintain a good position on the court, and so be ready to execute your next shot. If not, it will be a good bet that the next ball that comes over the net to you will be a winner for your opponent. Often you will see players run like mad to reach a return, but they will not try and return to a good court position with the same enthusiasm. You should always get into a good position, and as quickly as possible.

You will hear the expression 'playing the percentage' a lot these days. It is a very important part of the game but, quite simply, it means playing a shot that gives you more of a chance of winning a point. Looking at it logically, if you do not put the ball back into play then you have no chance of playing a percentage whatsoever. Putting your first service into play gives you a greater percentage chance of success than relying upon your second serve. You must always put your return of serve into play; don't, and once again you have no chance of a percentage.

Always put your first volley into play – again, this gives you an advantage. And finally, if you are in doubt which shot to play, then play the one you are happiest with. It may not be a winning shot, but if there was any doubt in your mind, then it would most probably have been a *losing* shot anyway.

All the above should also be considered when playing the doubles game. Obviously court positions are considerably different, and it is vital that you know where your team-mate is at all times. You should work out a pre-determined plan of what part of the court each of you should take when serving or receiving. There are so many different combinations of court position in doubles play. Both players may take an attacking position at the net on either side of the court, or one may take the attacking position while the other defends at the rear of the court, and so on.

Basic tactics to remember in doubles play are: (a) it is a team game – don't forget you have a partner on court; (b) try and get to the net before your opponents; (c) keep the ball low over the net, particularly when returning service. Lobs in the doubles game are often losing strokes, because one, or both, opposing players stand a good chance of getting to the ball. Most good rallies in doubles are played when all four players are close to the net and balls are played low.

Like the singles game, it is important to win your service game, to keep the ball in play, and to play the percentage game. Weaknesses should also be exploited, just as in singles. But in doubles there will inevitably be a weak partner; his or her weaknesses should be exploited to the full.

USEFUL
ADDRESSES

Lawn Tennis Association
Barons Court
West Kensington
London W14 9EG
01-385-2366

Lawn Tennis Association of Australia
Box 343
South Yarra
Victoria 3141
Australia

British Women's Tennis Association
c/o Beaconsfield School of Lawn Tennis
Beaconsfield
Bucks
04946-4744

Canadian Tennis Association
3111 Steeles Avenue West
Downsview
Ontario
M3J 3H2
Canada

Ceskoslovenska Tenisova Asociace
Ostrov Stvanice 38
170 00 Prague 7
C. Sprotsvaz Prague

Federation Francaise de Tennis
Stade Roland Garros
2 Avenue Gordon Bennett
75016 Paris
France

Duetscher Tennis Bund e.V.
Hallerstrasse 89
2000 Hamburg 13

All India Lawn Tennis Association
D-3/7 Asaf Ali Road
New Delhi 110
001, India

International Tennis Federation
Paliser Road
Barons Court
London
W14 9EN
01-381-8060

Tennis Ireland
54 Wellington Road
Ballsbridge
Dublin 4

Monica Seles keeps her eye on the ball despite having to run hard across court to meet the shot.

TENNIS

Federazione Italiana Tennis
Viale Tiziano 70
00196 Rome
Italy

New Zealand Lawn Tennis Association
PO Box 11541
Manners Street
Wellington
New Zealand

The South African Tennis Union
PO Box 2211
Johannesburg 2000
South Africa

Svenska Tennis Forbundet
Lidingovagen 75
S 115 37 Stockholm
Sweden

United States Tennis Association
12th Floor
1212 Avenue of the Americas
New York
NY10036
0101-212-302-3322

RULES CLINIC

INDEX

ball
  caught on racket   41
  changing during
      tie-breaker   44
  damaged   41
  hitting ball on ground   43
  hitting net during rally   41
  hitting net post   41
  hitting permanent fixture after
      good shot   41
  hitting permanent fixture after
      serve   39
  missed at serve   40
break, timing of   44

doubles
  receiving serve out of
      turn   39
  serving out of turn   39

feet, position at service   43

hindrance to playing shot   43

let
  for ball hitting net   41

for damaged ball   41
for hindrance   43

net
  ball blown back over   41
  ball hitting during rally   41
  hit by flying racket   41
  racket going over in follow
      through   42
net post, ball hitting   41

permanent fixtures
  ball hitting after shot   42
  definition of   43
  service hitting   39
player's position
  when hitting ball   42
  when serving   43

racket
  accidental damage to   41
  catching ball on   41
  deliberate damage to   41
  going over net in follow
      through   42

slipping from hand and hitting
      net   41

service
  deciding not to hit ball   40
  failing to hit ball   40
  from wrong end   39
  from wrong half of court   39
  hitting permanent fixture   39
  out of turn   39
  position of feet   43
  time limit between end of point
      and next serve   44
service, change of, going to
      wrong end at   39
service, in doubles, wrong player
      serving   39
service, receiving   44
  out of turn   39

tie-break, changing ball in   44

wrong end
  going to at change over   39
  serving from   39
wrong half, serving from   39

INDEX

Ace   23
All-England Lawn Tennis &
    Croquet Club,
    Wimbledon   9,10
Australian Championships
    9,10

backhand   23
    double-handed
        48,49,58,60–1
    drive   56–8
    grip   47,48,49
    volley   60–1,65
ball   18–19
    damaged   41
    in or out   33–4
Borg, Bjorn   12
Borotra, Jean   10
Brugnon, Jacques   10
Budge, Donald   10

championships   9,10,12
clothing   19–22
Cochet, Henri   10
Connolly, Maureen   10
court   12–13,14–17
Court, Margaret   10
cross court shots   23

Davis, Dwight F.   10
Davis Cup   10,12
deuce   23,24,34
Dod, Lottie   10
doubles   9,24,37–8
    mixed   9
    order of service in 37–8,39
    tie-breaker in   38
drop shot   24,72,73

fault   24,32,39–40
    double   24,31,32
    foot   24,31

forehand   24
    drive   55–6,73
    grip   46–8
French tennis and
    players   9,10,12

Gore, Spencer William   9
Grand Slam   9,10
grip   46–9
    advanced service   49,54
    backhand   47,48
    eastern forehand   46–8
    two-handed   48,49,58

International Lawn Tennis
    Federation   10

judges   25,36–7

King, Billie Jean   10

Lacoste, René   10
Laver, Rod   10,12
Lendl, Ivan   12
Lenglen, Suzanne   10,12
let   24–5,37,41,42,43
linesmen (judges)   25,36–7
lob   25,68–9,73

match point   25
misconduct   33

Navratilova, Martina   10,12
net   16–17
net cord   24–5

passing shot   26
Perry, Fred   10
playing surfaces   12,14
points, winning & losing   32–3
    see also scoring
Perera, J.B.   8

racket   8,13,17–18
    damage to   41
    grip   46–9
referee   26,36

scoring   23,24,25,26,34–6
seeding   10,26
service   26,30–2,39,43,51–5
    grip   49,54
    in doubles   37–8,39
    spin in   75
    technique   51–5
service, receiving   32,37–8,44
slice   27
smash   27,66–7
spin   73–5

tactics   75–6
tennis
    court   12–13,14–17
    equipment   17–22
    origin & development   8–13
    professionalism in   10–12
    technique   46–75
    terminology   23–9
tennis, real   8
tie-breaker   12,27,34–6,38,44

umpire   27,33,36–7
US Championships   9,10
US Lawn Tennis Association   9

volley   29,41,32,58–9
    backhand   60–1
    deep   23
    half   24,59–60,61,64
    stop   27
Wills-Moody, Helen   10
Wimbledon Championships
    9–10,12
Wingfield, Major Walter
    Clopton   8–9